INSIDE
HURRICANES

By Mary Kay Carson

STERLING

New York / London
www.sterlingpublishing.com/kids

STERLING and the distinctive Sterling logo are registered trademarks of
Sterling Publishing Co., Inc.

Library of Congress Cataloging-in-Publication Data Available

Lot#:
2 4 6 8 10 9 7 5 3 1
05/10
Published by Sterling Publishing Co., Inc.
387 Park Avenue South, New York, NY 10016
© 2010 by Mary Kay Carson
Distributed in Canada by Sterling Publishing
c/o Canadian Manda Group, 165 Dufferin Street
Toronto, Ontario, Canada M6K 3H6
Distributed in the United Kingdom by GMC Distribution Services
Castle Place, 166 High Street, Lewes, East Sussex, England BN7 1XU
Distributed in Australia by Capricorn Link (Australia) Pty. Ltd.
P.O. Box 704, Windsor, NSW 2756, Australia

Sterling ISBN 978-1-4027-5880-5 (hardcover)
978-1-4027-7780-6 (flexibound)

For information about custom editions, special sales, premium and
corporate purchases, please contact Sterling Special Sales
Department at 800-805-5489 or specialsales@sterlingpublishing.com.

Designed by Celia Fuller

- -

IMAGE CREDITS: From "Hurricane Intensity and Eyewall Replacement."
Reprinted with permission from AAAS.: 41 (bottom); © Corbis: 4; © Smiley
N. Pool/Dallas; Morning News/Corbis: 35; © David Frazier/Corbis: 34;
© Jim McDonald/CORBIS: 23 (top); © Will & Deni McIntyre/CORBIS: 23
(middle); © Reuters/CORBIS: 28 (right foreground); © J.P. MOCZULSKI/
Reuters/Corbis: 25; © HENRY; ROMERO/Reuters/Corbis: 22; © Blake
Sell/Reuters/Corbis: 24 (middle); © Michael Macor/San Francisco Chronicle/
Corbis: 36; © Ted Soqui/Corbis: 24 (bottom); © Bernard Bisson/Sygma/Corbis:
30–31; © Michel Jauzac/Sygma/Corbis: 23–24; © Mike Theiss/Corbis: 9,
back flap; © US Air Force - digital version c/Science Faction/Corbis: 18–19;
© Rungroj Yongrit/epa/Corbis: 5; Image by Robert A. Rohde, Global Warming
Art: 7–8; Mark Gong: 37 (bottom foreground); © iStockphoto.com/
"ROBERTO ADRIAN": 6–7 (background); © iStockphoto.com/"Pgiam":
45, 46; © iStockphoto.com/"Roel Smart": 29 (bottom background),
28 (right background), 31 (right background), 37 (bottom background), 40
(background), 44 (bottom); © iStockphoto.com/"Mark Winfrey": 43 (left
foreground and background); © iStockphoto.com/"Lisa F. Young": 43 (right);

Maps and Diagrams by Joe LeMonnier: 6–7 (foreground), 11, 16/21, 17, 20,
28 (left), 29 (top foreground), 31 (top left), 33 (foreground), 37 (top
foreground), 38 (foreground), 39; Library of Congress: 26 (foreground and
background), 29 (top background); NASA: 8 (background), 27, 31 (right
foreground), 33 (background), 42; NASA image by Jesse Allen, Earth
Observatory: 2–3; Jacques Descloitres, MODIS Land Rapid Response Team,
NASA/GSFC: 8 (foreground); NASA/Goddard Space Flight Center/Stöckli,
Nelson, Hasler: 47, 48, back cover (foreground); NASA/Goddard Space
Flight Center Scientific Visualization Studio: 10; NASA image by Jeff
Schmaltz, MODIS Rapid Response Team: 13, 14; Animation by Robert
Simmon, based on data provided by NOAA and archived by the NASA
GOES Project Science Team: 37 (top background), 38 (background),
39 (top background); National Oceanic and Atmospheric Administration
(NOAA): 1, 12, 15, 29 (bottom foreground), 32, back cover (background);
Jeff Masters, NOAA: 40 (foreground); Valerie Sigler: 44 (top left and right);
Courtesy Wikimedia Commons/jamesdale10: 41 (top); Front cover art:
Burton McNeely/Getty Images

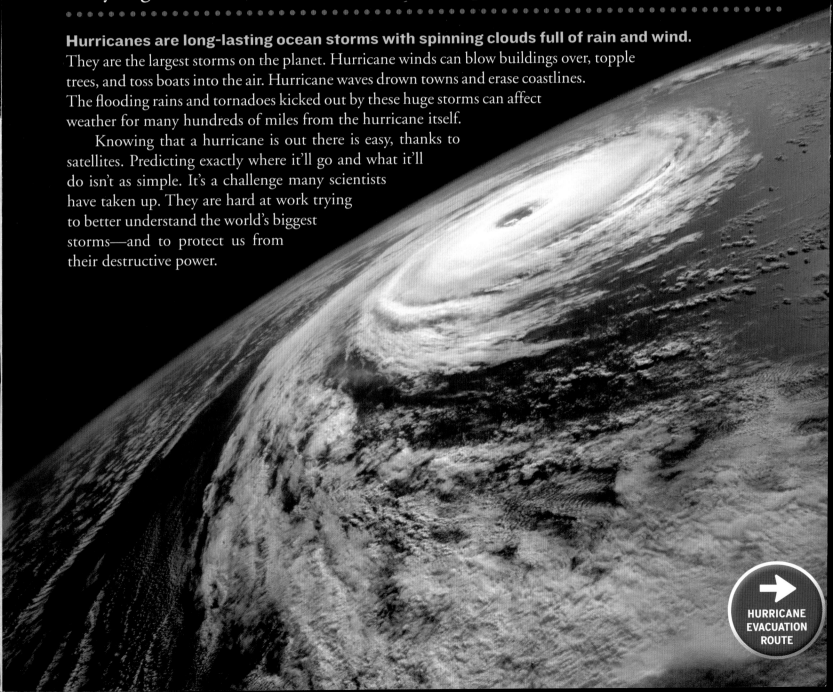

Hurricane's Coming!

Hurricanes are disasters that have called ahead to say they're coming. Hurricanes don't come out of nowhere. Scientists watch the storms develop and wander across an ocean for days or weeks. They're global weather events, visible from space!

Hurricanes are long-lasting ocean storms with spinning clouds full of rain and wind. They are the largest storms on the planet. Hurricane winds can blow buildings over, topple trees, and toss boats into the air. Hurricane waves drown towns and erase coastlines. The flooding rains and tornadoes kicked out by these huge storms can affect weather for many hundreds of miles from the hurricane itself.

Knowing that a hurricane is out there is easy, thanks to satellites. Predicting exactly where it'll go and what it'll do isn't as simple. It's a challenge many scientists have taken up. They are hard at work trying to better understand the world's biggest storms—and to protect us from their destructive power.

→ **HURRICANE EVACUATION ROUTE**

Where and When Do Hurricanes Happen?

Hurricanes start over oceans near the equator—the tropical oceans. In fact, the scientific name for these storms is *tropical cyclone*. In North America, tropical cyclones are called hurricanes. But these same storms go by other names in other parts of the world. No matter what they're called, hurricanes are fueled by warm seawater—at least 80°F (27°C). Whenever and wherever the world's oceans are this warm is where hurricanes happen.

Stormy Gods

The word *hurricane* came from native Central Americans. *Hurakan* was the name of a Maya creator god and *Hurican* was what the Carib people called the god of evil.

Cyclone Nargis was a huge, devastating, and deadly storm. It hit the country of Myanmar in 2008 and killed at least 146,000 people. The tropical cyclone began in the Indian Ocean, so it was called a cyclone.

5

Where Do Hurricanes Happen?

TROPICAL CYCLONES AROUND THE WORLD

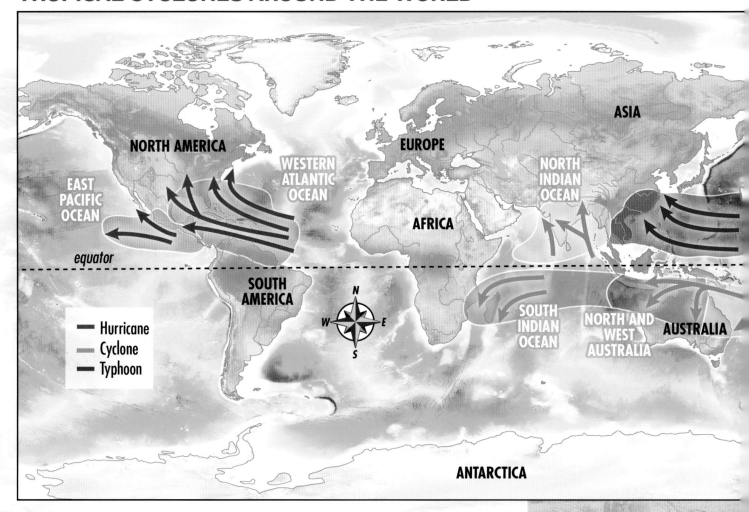

Every year an average of one hundred tropical cyclones form around the world. Most happen in one of the seven colored ocean regions shown. *Tropical cyclone* is the universal, or generic, name for these monster storms. They're also called by other names depending on where they happen. Those on both sides of North America and Central America are called hurricanes. The same storms in the Indian Ocean are called cyclones. Typhoons happen in the northern Pacific Ocean off the coast of eastern Asia. Which ocean has the most storms? Which hemisphere?

Contents

Hurricane's Coming!   4

Where and When Do Hurricanes Happen?   5

Why and How Do Hurricanes Happen?   10

How Bad Is It? Sizing Up Hurricanes   22

Hurricanes to Remember   26

Storm Scientists in Action   38

Hurricane Safety   43

Hurricane Tracker Words to Know   45

Bibliography   45

Source Notes   45

Find Out More   46

Index   48

How to Read This Book

This book is different from most you've read. Many of its pages fold out—or flip up! To know where to read next, follow arrows like these ⬆ and look for page numbers like these 🌀 to help you find your place. Happy exploring!

Explosive Energy

During its life, a hurricane can use up as much energy as 10,000 nuclear bombs. Ka-boom!

HURRICANE
EVACUATION
ROUTE

When Is Tropical Cyclone Season?

In general, it's open season for tropical cyclones whenever ocean waters are at their warmest—summer and early fall. Hurricane season in North and Central America is June through November. Cyclones in the North Indian Ocean usually happen in May and November. The South Indian Ocean and Australia have their tropical cyclone season from December to March. East Asian typhoons can strike all year, but they are most likely to form June through December.

When Do Hurricanes Happen?

Hurricanes peak in the Atlantic Ocean in August and September. That's when the water is at its warmest.

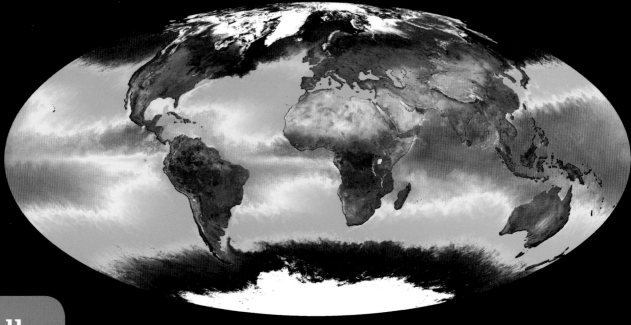

-2   5   10   15   20 25 30 35
°C

This map shows the sea surface temperatures across the world during May 2001.

Oddball Event

No one thought hurricanes hit South America until 2004. That year, a weak hurricane named Catarina battered Brazil. Can you find its looping track on the map?

Tracing Storm Paths

TROPICAL STORM TRACKS

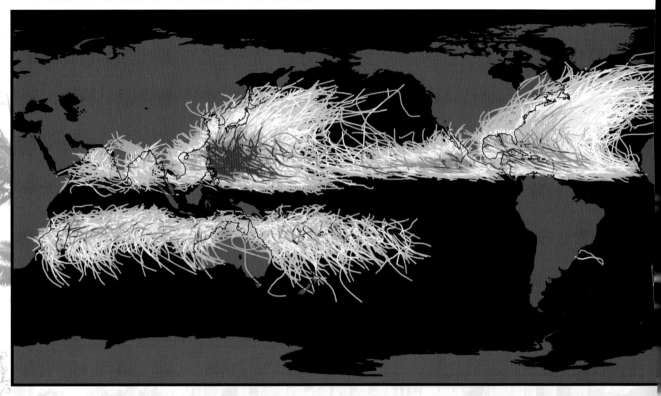

Each ribbon-like streak on this map is the path of a single tropical cyclone. The map shows the paths of all the recorded tropical cyclones—hurricanes, typhoons, and cyclones—that happened around the world during approximately the past 150 years. Red streaks are the most powerful storms, yellow are medium strength, and blue are the weakest.

The map tells us a lot about where tropical storms happen—and why. See that biggest, reddest patch off the coast of Southeast Asia? Average ocean temperatures there are the highest on Earth. All that heat cooks up lots of storms. In contrast, chilly currents cool down the Southwest Pacific and South Atlantic oceans. This leaves the west coast of South America and southern Africa practically free of tropical cyclones.

Why and How Do Hurricanes Happen?

Hurricanes are Earth's biggest and most destructive storms. These gigantic spiraling storms from the tropics are hundreds of miles across. Hurricanes can be as wide as Kansas and Nebraska combined! They have the power to churn a million cubic miles of atmosphere every second, dumping more than 2 trillion gallons (7,570,824kl) of rain in a day, and unleashing winds that pack a punch. A 150-mile-per-hour (mph), or 241 kilometer-per-hour (km/h), hurricane wind has the slamming push of 11 tons (10 mt) of pressure. That's like a herd of elephants coming toward you at race-car speed. It has enough force to smash a house or turn a tree into a missile.

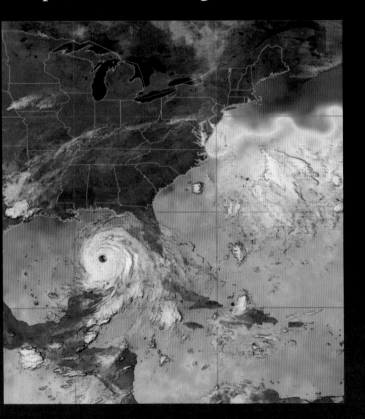

If the energy a hurricane makes in just one day could be turned into electricity, it could power the entire United States for half a year. Hurricanes have so much power and energy that they affect the whole planet. Hurricanes, typhoons, and other tropical cyclones help Earth balance its temperature. These storms move some of the heat from the tropics out toward the cooler areas around the North and South Poles. Hurricanes are worldwide weather events. Why do they happen? How are these monster storms created?

● ●

This is Hurricane Katrina heading toward Louisiana and Mississippi in late August 2005. The colors in the ocean represent temperature. Orange and red areas are 82°F (28°C) and hotter. This is plenty warm enough for hurricanes to form—and be fueled. Katrina strengthened after crossing into the Gulf of Mexico's warmer waters.

Hurricane Ingredients

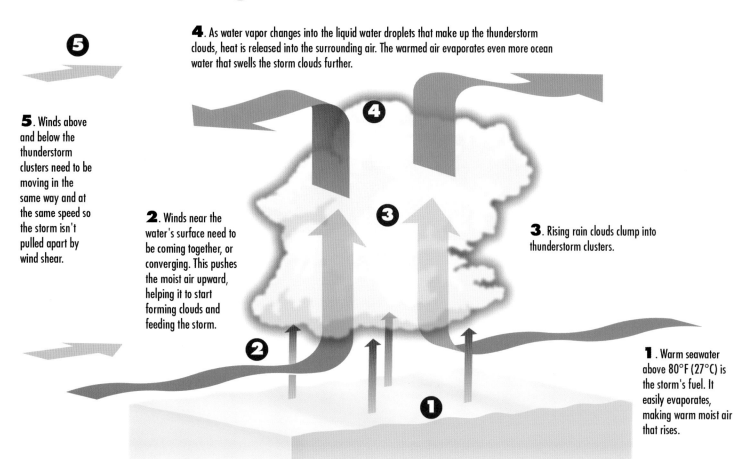

5

4. As water vapor changes into the liquid water droplets that make up the thunderstorm clouds, heat is released into the surrounding air. The warmed air evaporates even more ocean water that swells the storm clouds further.

5. Winds above and below the thunderstorm clusters need to be moving in the same way and at the same speed so the storm isn't pulled apart by wind shear.

2. Winds near the water's surface need to be coming together, or converging. This pushes the moist air upward, helping it to start forming clouds and feeding the storm.

3. Rising rain clouds clump into thunderstorm clusters.

1. Warm seawater above 80°F (27°C) is the storm's fuel. It easily evaporates, making warm moist air that rises.

4

3

2

1

Hurricanes don't happen in an instant, like a tornado or a lightning strike. Even the fiercest hurricane was once a small thunderstorm. A storm only grows into a hurricane if all the right ingredients come together.

First on the ingredients list is heat. Heat is what fuels a hurricane. Where does a growing storm in the tropics get heat? It comes from deep, warm ocean waters. Warm water easily evaporates into water vapor, like in a steamy shower. This evaporation creates another needed atmospheric ingredient—moist, humid air. When warm, moist air rises, it forms rain clouds. Rain clouds are made up of very tiny droplets of water. They're so small that more than a million would fit into a teaspoon! Rising water vapor cools off and forms these tiny droplets. The heat lost by the cooling water vapor goes into the air. The warmed-up air evaporates even more ocean water, swelling the rain clouds further.

Another important ingredient is the right kind of winds. Winds near the ocean's surface have to come together, or converge. Converging winds push the growing rain clouds upward, creating clusters of thunderstorms. The thunderstorm clusters keep growing if the winds above and below them are all moving in the same way and at the same speed. This means there isn't much wind shear. Wind shear would pull apart the thunderstorms. If all these ingredients come together, the cooked-up cluster of thunderstorms is called a tropical disturbance. It's the official name for a storm that can grow into a tropical cyclone. A tropical disturbance is a hurricane seed.

Stage 3
Tropical Storm

Gaining Speed:

If moist, warm waters continue to feed the storm, it grows bigger. The air inside the larger storm rises faster, pulling in more new fuel from the ocean's surface—and creating faster winds. The fuel-gobbling storm takes on a more defined, dense, round, and spinning shape. Once the spiraling storm's winds reach 39 mph (63km/h), it's declared a tropical storm. In North America, the National Hurricane Center gives the tropical storm a name. Tropical storms can dump flooding rains and have powerful winds from 39 to 73 mph (63 to 117km/h).

HURRICANE
EVACUATION
ROUTE

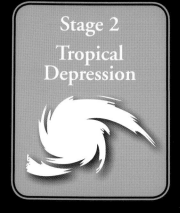

Stage 2
Tropical Depression

Fueling Up:

While moving over warm Atlantic Ocean waters, the storm grows wider and taller, fueled by moist, humid air. Warm air full of water vapor over the ocean's surface rises into the storm. Once that rising water vapor hits cooler air higher up it forms clouds. Cloud-making releases heat, which warms up the surrounding air, making the storm rise more—and faster. As air within the storm keeps rising like smoke up a chimney, air at the ocean's surface is sucked in toward the storm. That rushing air is wind. Because Earth is spinning, those winds curve as they move inward, and the storm starts to swirl. The spinning storm is now a tropical depression with heavy rain and winds from 23 to 38 miles per hour (mph), or 37 to 61 kilometers per hour (km/h). Only one in ten tropical depressions grows into a hurricane.

Reason for Rotation

The Coriolis effect is the term used to describe why our spinning planet sets storms rotating and creates a hurricane's swirl.

HURRICANE EVACUATION ROUTE

Weather Expert

A meteorologist is a weather scientist.

How Do Hurricanes Develop?

Developing storms with the right ingredients go through four stages on their way to becoming full-blown hurricanes.

Out of Africa:

A tropical disturbance is a cluster of growing thunderstorms over warm ocean waters near the equator. It can have heavy rain but no strong wind. A tropical disturbance is what gives birth to a hurricane. Most tropical disturbances that grow into large hurricanes begin life as thunderstorm clusters coming from western Africa. Meteorologists keep a close eye on that side of the Atlantic Ocean during hurricane season. These patches of thunderstorms leaving Africa's west coast are often called African easterly waves. A thunderstorm cluster moves up and down like a wave as trade winds carry it eastward all the way across the Atlantic Ocean toward the Americas.

Stage 1
Tropical Disturbance

Eye Opening:

Strong winds whip up the warm ocean water, evaporating it faster, creating even more moist, warm air to fuel the hungry storm. Air rising into the storm speeds up, creating faster winds at the ocean's surface as air is pulled up into the storm. When winds reach 74 mph (119km/h) or faster, the storm is declared a hurricane (or typhoon, cyclone, or tropical cyclone). It is at least 50,000 feet (15,240m) high and 125 miles (201km) wide at this point. A column of warm air spirals up in the center of the hurricane, creating a ring of tall thunderstorms with the storm's strongest winds. The super fast winds spin open a hole free of clouds called the eye.

EARTH'S CHANGING CLIMATE
Will Hurricanes Increase?

Our planet is warming up. Earth's average temperature has been rising for decades. Scientists agree that human-caused pollution from burning coal, oil, and gas causes global warming. Rising temperatures change our planet's climate. Scientists predict global climate change will melt ice caps, raise the level of the sea, and bring more extreme weather like droughts, floods, and storms. Does this mean more hurricanes, too?

"If there is an increase in sea-surface temperatures, there will be an increase in hurricane activity," explains climate scientist Kevin Trenberth. Hurricanes and other kinds of tropical cyclones are global weather events. They are part of Earth's system for keeping a more even temperature. The tropics build up a lot of heat. Hurricanes move some of that heat away from the tropics, sending it out toward Earth's chilly poles. These giant ocean storms are a way for our planet to shift heat around—balancing its temperature. "If global warming is happening, how can hurricanes not be affected?" says Trenberth. "It's part of the overall system."

"Sea-surface temperatures have gone up because of global warming," says Trenberth. Scientists estimate that tropical oceans have already warmed during the past several decades by one-half to one degree. Warmer water means more fuel for hurricanes. Will extra fuel create additional hurricanes each year or just jumbo-size the ones that do happen? The overall number of hurricanes may or may not increase—no one knows yet. Some scientists argue that warmer water could create more wind shear, which can keep ocean storms from growing into tropical cyclones.

Most scientists do think that warmer oceans will likely make the hurricanes that do happen *stronger*. Warmer water puts more water vapor into the air, boosting a storm's growth. Computer simulations, called models, predict that tropical cyclone winds will speed up as seawaters warm. Faster winds build bigger storms that let loose more flooding rain. "When it rains, it pours much more so now than it did a few years ago," adds Trenberth. More intense hurricanes shove higher storm surges ashore, too. Add that fact to the possibility of rising sea levels along the coasts as the ice caps melt. It leaves many heavily-populated areas at risk of disastrous flooding. More destruction due to hurricanes seems a certain part of our warmer future.

Rising Oceans

Florida is very vulnerable to rising oceans from climate change. Some 4,730 square miles (12,251 square km) of land are less than 5 feet (1.5m) above sea level.

Deadly Storm Tides

A full-blown hurricane churning across the ocean is a powerful force. Ships make sure to avoid its whipped-up waves, wind, and pounding rain. Meteorologists track its path closely. However, hurricanes, typhoons, and tropical cyclones do their worst damage out of the water. When a hurricane hits a coast or an island, it's said to be making landfall. At landfall, a hurricane's wild winds rip up houses, trees, and power lines. Its rainbands can swamp towns and set down twisters far from its eye. But it's the storm surge, with its flooding power, that's the most dangerous.

The storm surge is a giant mound of seawater. It is caused by a rapid rise in sea level underneath the hurricane. The hurricane's intense winds pile up most of the water. The low pressure around the storm's eye can also add to the storm surge. How? The low-pressure area adds extra seawater into the storm surge by pulling it upward, like sucking on a straw to pick up a napkin. As the hurricane makes landfall, it takes the storm surge with it. The mound of water is shoved onto land, sending flooding seawater ashore.

A storm surge can be more than 20 feet (6 meters) high and flood hundreds of miles of shoreline. If the coast is already at high tide, the storm surge becomes extra-big and is called a storm tide. Storm surges and storm tides flood towns, completely cover islands, and wash away beaches. Wind, rain, and tornadoes don't do nearly as much damage as the storm surge. Throughout history, storm surges have been the most deadly part of a hurricane—causing nine out of ten deaths.

While a hurricane drags in destruction on landfall, it also instantly begins to die. Why? On land a hurricane is cut off from its fuel—warm ocean water. If a hurricane keeps traveling inland, it quickly weakens into a tropical storm, then a tropical depression, and eventually dies. Only by heading back out to warm water to refuel will it strengthen and perhaps move on to strike elsewhere!

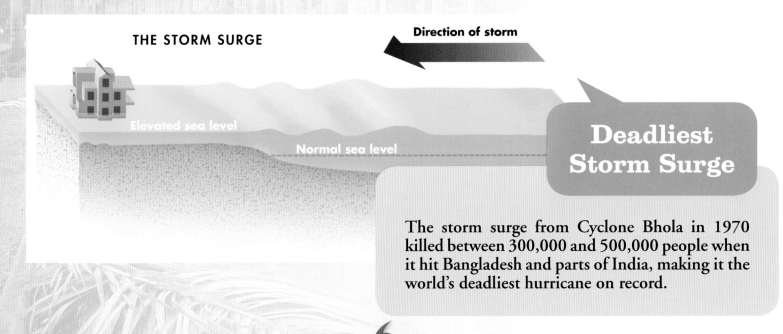

THE STORM SURGE

Direction of storm

Elevated sea level

Normal sea level

Deadliest Storm Surge

The storm surge from Cyclone Bhola in 1970 killed between 300,000 and 500,000 people when it hit Bangladesh and parts of India, making it the world's deadliest hurricane on record.

Hurricane Anatomy: Take a Look Inside the Storm

A hurricane is an amazing thing. It's like a machine that feeds itself. A hurricane will keep growing and strengthening as long as it has fuel—heat from warm water.

EYE

The eye is usually between 20–40 miles (32–64km) across and has no clouds overhead. It's a long tube of calm all the way to the sea—like a hole in the center of water swirling down a drain.

RAINBANDS

These curved bands are packed with thunderstorm clouds. They can reach hundreds of miles from the eye and produce rain, lightning, and, sometimes, tornadoes.

SINKING COOL AIR

The winds are always strongest to the "right" of the direction a hurricane is traveling. So a northward storm's fastest winds are to the east, an eastward storm's fastest winds are to the south, etc.

DIRECTION HURRICANE IS MOVING

HURRICANE EVACUATION ROUTE

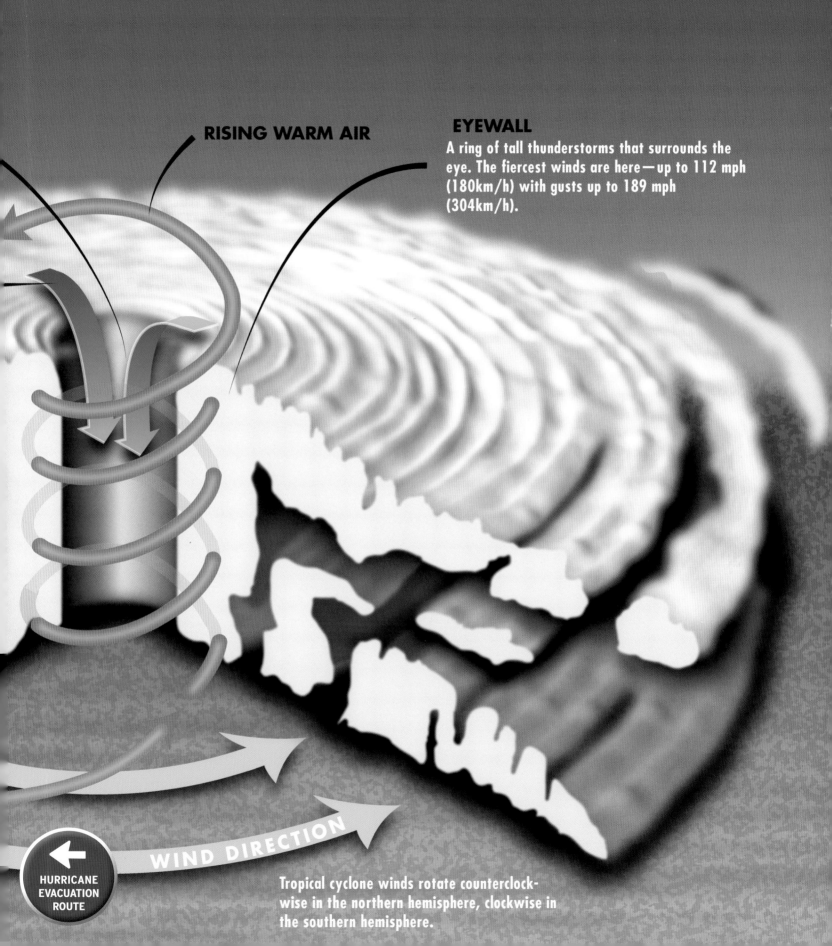

RISING WARM AIR

EYEWALL
A ring of tall thunderstorms that surrounds the eye. The fiercest winds are here—up to 112 mph (180km/h) with gusts up to 189 mph (304km/h).

WIND DIRECTION

HURRICANE EVACUATION ROUTE

Tropical cyclone winds rotate counterclockwise in the northern hemisphere, clockwise in the southern hemisphere.

Hurricane Activity
Measuring Pressure

The lower the atmospheric or air pressure, the stronger the storm. A barometer is a weather instrument that measures air pressure. Here's a simple barometer you can make to measure air pressure around you.

You'll Need

empty metal coffee can
large balloon
duct tape
toothpick

clear tape or glue
drinking straw
lined index card

To Do

1. **Cut the neck off a large balloon.** Stretch the balloon top tightly over the coffee can. Use duct tape to secure it to the can. It needs an airtight seal!
2. **Tape or glue the toothpick to one end of the straw.** The toothpick should be attached in a straight line with the straw. This will be the barometer's indicator needle.
3. **Lay the end of the straw without the toothpick on top of the balloon-covered can.** Use a single strip of clear tape (or glue) to attach the straw onto the balloon top, as shown.

4. **Set your barometer indoors in a still area where the temperature doesn't change much.** Don't set it in a sunny window or a drafty spot. (Note: This kind of barometer's readings isn't accurate if the temperature changes.)
5. **Number the lines on an index card.** Then tape it to a wall or cabinet next to the barometer so that its indicator (the toothpick) points toward the lines in the middle of the card.
6. **Wait a few hours to take a first reading.** The toothpick will rise and fall as changes in air pressure contract and expand the balloon, moving the straw. You can track how air pressure changes with sunny, cloudy, rainy, or stormy weather by recording the toothpick's location over time.

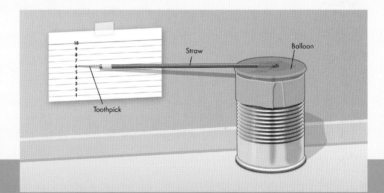

Under Air Pressure

Earth is surrounded by a blanket of air—the atmosphere. The atmosphere's weight pushes down on Earth's land and ocean, like blankets stacked on a bed. This pushing force is called atmospheric pressure, or air pressure. Atmospheric pressure changes with height—and with temperature. Warm air weighs less than cool air. Warm air is less dense, and, therefore, lighter, because its fast-moving molecules spread out. Being lighter is why warm air naturally rises—and has a lower pressure.

Areas of air with low pressure cause storms as the air rises, and its water vapor forms clouds. A hurricane's lowest pressure is in and around the eye. This is where less dense, warming air is rising up into the storm. The lower the air pressure in the eye of a hurricane, the faster and stronger the outside air rushes in—to make even faster winds. The strongest hurricanes have the lowest pressure (see pages 23–24). Low pressure also causes the sea level below the storm to rise, adding to the flooding storm surge.

Millions of people live along the hurricane-whipped Atlantic and Gulf coasts of the United States. Many of those coastal areas aren't much higher than sea level. That makes them especially vulnerable to storm surges—and rising sea levels. This photograph shows a New Orleans neighborhood under water. It was flooded by Hurricane Katrina.

HOW BAD IS IT?
Sizing Up Hurricanes

A hurricane is a gigantic storm with rain, low pressure, and a dangerous storm surge upon landfall. But it's the hurricane's winds that define it. Only when constant winds are measured at 74 mph (119km/h) or higher is a tropical storm declared a true hurricane. Meteorologists use a hurricane's wind speeds to measure its strength, too. Hurricanes are rated from Category 1 (weakest) to Category 5 (strongest) based on their constant wind speeds—not just single gusts. The hurricane rating system is called the Saffir-Simpson Hurricane Scale. Want to see it? Flip up the page on the right side!

Storm Scale's Namesakes

Building engineer Herbert Saffir and then National Hurricane Center director Bob Simpson developed the scale named after them in 1969.

Naming the Storm

How can you tell one storm from another? You give it a name. Tornadoes are often named after the places where they cause destruction, such as the Oklahoma City Tornado. Winter storms usually are named for a year, such as the Blizzard of 1977. Hurricanes are different. They are given people's names—such as Bob, Kay, Julio, or Rita.

Hurricane naming has a long tradition. Unlike other kinds of storms, hurricanes can last weeks and travel thousands of miles during their lives. We get to know them, scientists track them, and calling them by name makes it easier to talk about them. For hundreds of years, Latin Americans named storms after the saint's day of their landfall, like Hurricane San Felipe. By 1900, some storm trackers were giving tropical storms women's names. Every year since 1953, meteorologists have created a list of twenty-one names in alphabetical order for hurricanes. These lists started including men's names in 1979. Different name lists for tropical cyclones are used in regions of the Pacific Ocean where the storms are called typhoons and cyclones.

FOREVER RETIRED ATLANTIC HURRICANE NAMES

If a storm is especially costly or deadly, its name is taken off any future lists forever. The list of retired hurricane names reads like a disaster story full of bad memories. Do you recognize or remember any of the storms on the list? (The hurricane's year is in parentheses.) Is your name here?

AGNES (1972)	CONNIE (1955)	GILBERT (1988)	KEITH (2000)	MITCH (1998)
ALICIA (1983)	DAVID (1979)	GLORIA (1985)	KLAUS (1990)	OPAL (1995)
ALLEN (1980)	DENNIS (2005)	HATTIE (1961)	LENNY (1999)	RITA (2005)
ALLISON (2001)	DIANA (1990)	HAZEL (1954)	LILI (2002)	ROXANNE (1995)
ANDREW (1992)	DIANE (1955)	HILDA (1964)	LUIS (1995)	STAN (2005)
ANITA (1977)	DONNA (1960)	HORTENSE (1996)	MARILYN (1995)	WILMA (2005)
AUDREY (1957)	DORA (1964)	HUGO (1989)	MICHELLE (2001)	
BETSY (1965)	EDNA (1954)	INEZ (1966)		
BEULAH (1967)	ELENA (1985)	IONE (1955)		
BOB (1991)	ELOISE (1975)	IRIS (2001)		
CAMILLE (1969)	FABIAN (2003)	ISABEL (2003)		
CARLA (1961)	FIFI (1974)	ISIDORE (2002)		
CARMEN (1974)	FLORA (1963)	IVAN (2004)		
CAROL (1954)	FLOYD (1999)	JANET (1955)		
CESAR (1996)	FRAN (1996)	JEANNE (2004)		
CELIA (1970)	FRANCES (2004)	JOAN (1988)		
CHARLEY (2004)	FREDERIC (1979)	JUAN (2003)		
CLEO (1964)	GEORGES (1998)	KATRINA (2005)		

HURRICANE EVACUATION ROUTE

Greek Alphabet Soup

The year 2005 had so many hurricanes that meteorologists used up all the names on that year's list! Storms after the final name Wilma were given Greek alphabet letters as names—Alpha, Beta, Gamma, Delta, Epsilon, and Zeta.

SAFFIR-SIMPSON SCALE OF HURRICANE INTENSITY

Saffir-Simpson Category	Wind Speeds	Atmospheric Pressure	Storm Surge	Kind of Damage	What the Damage Looks Like
1	74-95 mph (119-153 km/h)	28.94-29.53 inches of mercury (inHg)	3-5 feet (0.9-1.5m)	**MINIMAL DAMAGE:** Buildings are mostly unharmed; mobile homes, trees, and signs are damaged. Some coastal road flooding, as well as dock and boat damage.	
2	96-110 mph (154-177 km/h)	28.50-28.93 (inHg)	6-8 feet (1.8-2.4m)	**MODERATE DAMAGE:** Some trees are blown down. Building roofs, doors, and windows are damaged. Coastal and low-lying escape routes flood 2-4 hours before arrival of the hurricane center. Small unsheltered boats break moorings.	
3	111-130 mph (179-209 km/h)	27.91-28.49 (inHg)	9-12 feet (2.7-3.7m)	**EXTENSIVE DAMAGE:** Some structural damage to small buildings. Mobile homes are destroyed. Large trees are blown down and signs destroyed. Flooding and wind destroy	

smaller buildings near the coast. Flat areas lower than 5 feet (1.5m) above sea level may be flooded inland 8 miles (13 km) or more.

4

131–155 mph

(211–249 km/h)

27.17–27.90 (inHg)

13–18 feet

(4–5.5m)

EXTREME DAMAGE: Roofs collapse on homes and small buildings. Low-lying escape routes may be cut off by rising water 3–5 hours before arrival of the center of the hurricane. Major damage to lower floors of buildings near the coast. Flat areas lower than 10 feet (3m) above sea level may be flooded, evacuation of residential areas as far inland as 6 miles (10km) may be necessary.

5

156 mph and above

(251km/h and above)

less than 27.17 (inHg)

higher than 18 feet

(5.5m)

CATASTROPHIC DAMAGE: Large buildings lose roofs. All trees blown down. Door and window glass shatters. Small buildings are overturned or blown away. Low-lying escape routes flood 3–5 hours before hurricane center arrives. Evacuation of areas as far inland as 5–10 miles (8–16km) may be required.

Hurricanes to Remember

Hurricanes happen every year, but not all storms are equal. Some hurricanes are so powerful, devastating, or destructive that they stand out from the rest.

The 1900 Galveston Hurricane

Where: Galveston, Texas • **When:** September 8, 1900
What: Category 4 at landfall • **How Bad:** 8,000 dead

A low-lying sandy island is a bad place to be during a hurricane. About half of the 37,000 people on the Texas island city of Galveston decided to head for the mainland when the sea turned rough in early September 1900. Sailors arriving at the port city warned that a strong storm was brewing in the Gulf of Mexico. Nearly half of those who stayed on the island would lose their lives once the hurricane hit.

The 1900 hurricane brought pounding waves and powerful winds. But it was the storm surge that drowned thousands. Even before daybreak on September 8, 1900, seawater was flooding beaches. People began fleeing to higher ground, but most of the island is less than nine feet (2.7m) above sea level. There was nowhere on the island to escape the eight-to-fifteen-foot (2.4–4.5m) storm tide. Even getting off the island became impossible after a steamship tossed by the waves destroyed the three bridges to the mainland. By 3:00 p.m., the entire island was under water, and gigantic waves rolled though downtown, knocking down tall buildings and sucking their occupants out to sea.

The hurricane that washed away Galveston never had a name, because tropical storms weren't officially named in 1900. The Galveston Hurricane changed history. Before this storm, Galveston was one of the richest cities in America, thanks to its shipping port. In the decades of rebuilding after the storm, much of the port traffic moved to a younger Texas town—Houston. The hurricane forever tarnished the "Jewel of Texas."

After the 1900 Galveston Hurricane, the city built a seventeen-foot high seawall more than ten miles long to protect the island against future storms. And it did, until Ike hit in 2008. The hurricane's storm tide topped the seawall, sending floodwaters into downtown Galveston. Ike damaged 75 percent of Galveston's homes and was the costliest natural disaster ever in Texas.

In this c.1900 photograph, survivors of the Galveston Hurricane rummage through rubble.

A DEADLY PATH

Before it hit Texas, Cuba experienced the Galveston Hurricane as a weaker tropical storm. Warm late summer Gulf of Mexico waters strengthened it to a Category 4 hurricane.

America's Most Deadly

The Galveston Hurricane was the deadliest in U.S. history by far. The next deadliest was the Okeechobee Hurricane of 1928 that killed at least 2,500 in Florida.

I WAS THERE!
A Deadly Forecast

Predicting the weather on Galveston in 1900 was the job of U.S. Weather Bureau scientist Isaac Cline. But Cline ignored warnings sent from Cuba and reports of sailors arriving from the Gulf of Mexico. He simply didn't believe that storms could be strong enough to flood the island.

By September 8, the scientist was beginning to change his mind. Waves were higher than anything he'd ever seen—or even heard about. He warned people to head for the mainland. By then, it was too late. The bridges were down and the water was rising. "The roofs of the houses and timbers were flying through the streets as though they were paper and it appeared suicidal to attempt a journey through the flying timbers," Cline wrote.

Isaac Cline claimed his own house would survive any hurricane. It did not. Powerful

Isaac Cline

waves and floating debris battered the home until it fell into the sea. "My residence went down with about 50 persons who had sought it out for safety and all but 18 were hurled into eternity," Cline reported. "I was nearly drowned and became unconscious, but recovered through being crushed by timbers and found myself clinging to my youngest child . . . we drifted for three hours. . . . There were two hours that we did not see a house nor any person, and from the swell, we inferred that we were drifting to sea." Actually, they'd drifted into downtown Galveston. Once the water went down, they were able to crawl into an upper floor of a tall building.

HURRICANE EVACUATION ROUTE

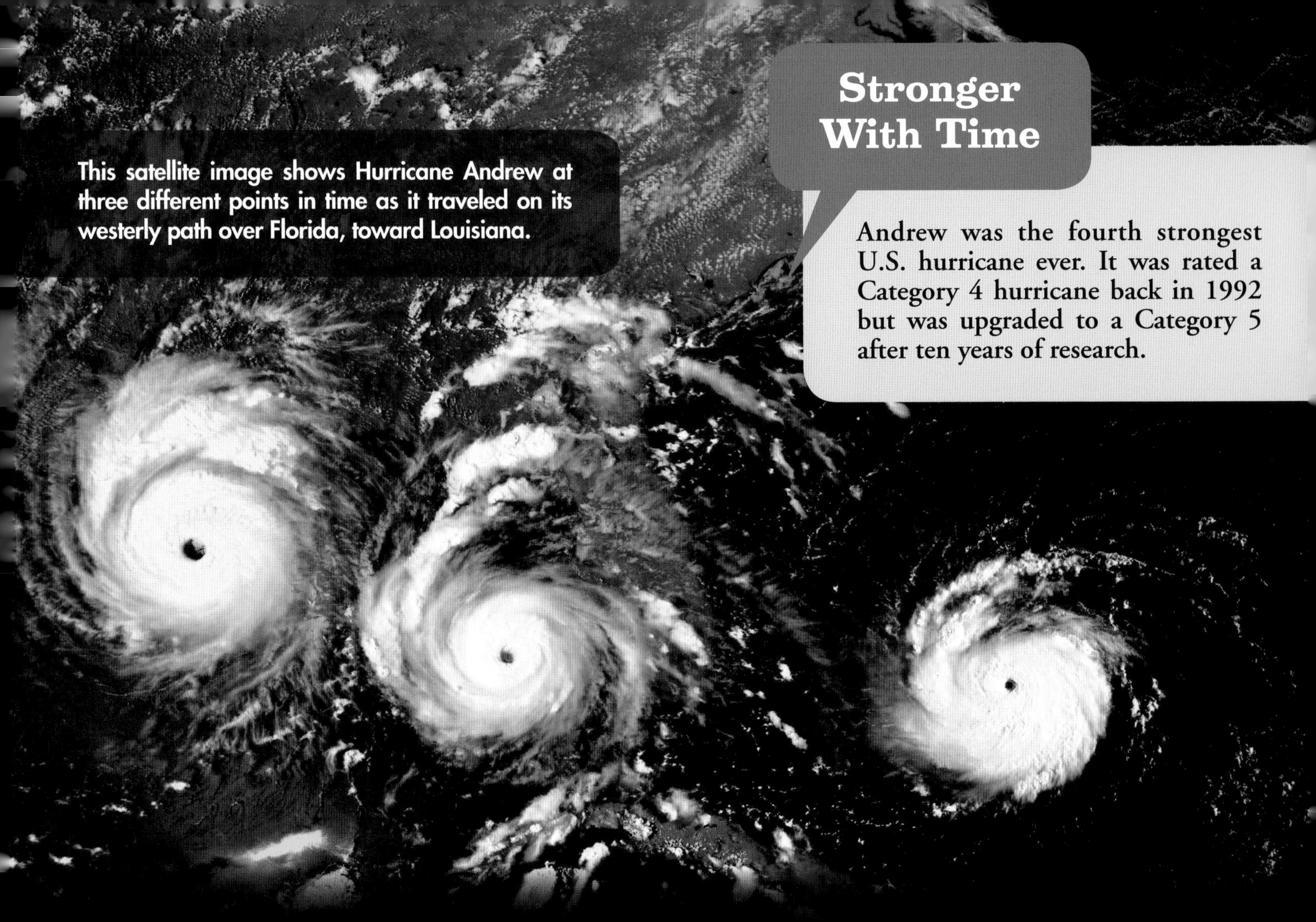

This satellite image shows Hurricane Andrew at three different points in time as it traveled on its westerly path over Florida, toward Louisiana.

Stronger With Time

Andrew was the fourth strongest U.S. hurricane ever. It was rated a Category 4 hurricane back in 1992 but was upgraded to a Category 5 after ten years of research.

Hurricane Andrew

Where: Southern Florida • **When:** August 24, 1992
What: Category 5 at landfall in Florida • **How Bad:** 26 dead

South Floridians thought they were ready for Hurricane Andrew. They'd stocked up on food, candles, and batteries. Homeowners had nailed plywood over windows and doors. But Andrew wasn't your average hurricane. It exploded onto land as a Category 5. Andrew's winds were tornado strength. Gusts topped 200 mph (322km/h). Andrew crushed thousands of mobile homes like cans. Its winds buzz-sawed through buildings. Boats were sucked off docks and thrown into backyards hundreds of feet away. People took shelter in bathtubs and under mattresses—like during a tornado. They peeked out and watched their roofs disappearing and walls tumbling down.

Hurricane Andrew wrecked whole Florida towns, including Homestead. Entire streets and subdivisions became piles of trash. The storm destroyed or damaged hundreds of thousands of homes and buildings. More than a quarter of a million people were left homeless.

Tropical storm Andrew was born on August 17, 1992. Andrew slowly churned northwest for five days before reaching hurricane strength. Wind shear nearly broke it apart on August 20! Once Andrew hit warmer water and the right winds, it began to strengthen—with a vengeance. A single day after becoming a hurricane, Andrew was a Category 4—and on its way to becoming a Category 5. After trashing Florida, Andrew headed northwest across the Gulf of Mexico. The hurricane then made a second landfall as a Category 3 storm on the central Louisiana coast.

Paying Andrew's Price

Andrew was the costliest hurricane in U.S. history by far when it happened in 1992. Of its $26.5 billion in damage, $1 billion of that damage was in Louisiana and the rest in Florida. Katrina surpassed Andrew as the costliest hurricane in 2005.

I WAS THERE!

A Long 105 Minutes

Florida middle school student Rachel Catz wrote about surviving Hurricane Andrew's "105 minutes of torture" for St. Petersburg's newspaper. She and her family huddled in a bedroom closet with a mattress over their heads as the hurricane roared over. "We heard the sliding glass door shatter, then three more big bay windows. The winds whistled as it took our precious belongings through the house, throwing some outside, turning over tables and chairs, stereos and couches."

After the storm passed, Catz and her family crawled out of the closet. "I couldn't believe my eyes. The couches were across the room, the dining-room table outside, wall units thrown to the floor." Andrew's fierce winds had shattered windows and tossed speakers through walls. "Of the whole block, my house was the worst. Everyone came, chopping down trees to make their way, to see if we were okay. We didn't have electricity for six days, a phone for two days."

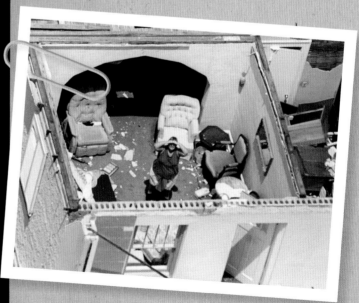

Many residents had their homes severely damaged by Hurricane Andrew. The violent storms ripped this woman's roof right off!

Hurricane Mitch

Where: Honduras, Nicaragua, Guatemala, and El Salvador
When: October 29–November 3, 1998 • **What:** Category 1 at landfall
How Bad: 11,000 dead; thousands missing

Mitch was barely a hurricane by the time it made landfall. On October 29, 1998, the Category 1 hurricane hit the coast of Honduras. The slow-moving storm's winds were weakening, but Mitch was a never-ending rainmaker. The sluggish storm continually dumped heavy rain as it came ashore on Central America. Even more rain was wrung out of the weakening hurricane as it neared the region's mountains—as much as three or more *feet* of rain. Towns flooded, roads disappeared, and bridges washed away. Then the rain-soaked mountains themselves began to move. Massive mudslides swept down the mountainsides. Families still in their homes were buried beneath the mud as whole hillsides gave way.

Flooding and mud-slides erased entire villages. The number of people killed is hard to know because so many were buried under tons of mud and never found. Mitch left at least 2 million people homeless. Many of Mitch's victims were already poor. The hurricane took what little they had—wooden shacks, vegetable gardens, and precious family members.

Central America's Deadliest

Mitch was the deadliest recorded hurricane to hit Central America and the deadliest in the Western Hemisphere in the past two centuries.

A SLOW-MOVING RAINMAKER

Mitch was a very powerful hurricane while at sea. Two days after becoming a hurricane on October 26, Mitch was a fierce Category 5.

Taken days after Hurricane Mitch ravaged Honduras, this photograph shows the streets of Tegucigalpa, the nation's capital city, covered in mud.

I WAS THERE!

Stuck in Mitch's Mud for Days

Rain brought by Hurricane Mitch soaked the ancient Casita Volcano in Nicaragua. An enormous mudslide plowed a wide path down the old volcanic mountain. The sliding earth thundered down on villages below, killing 2,000.

Among the dead was most of the Montoya Narvaez family. Seven-year-old Juan Pablo Montoya Narvaez lost his mother, father, and three of his siblings that day. The small curly-haired boy was lucky to survive. Mud surrounded his little body up to his neck. Juan Pablo was trapped but alive. Making matters worse were large fallen branches that hid him from sight. After two days, men from another village finally found him. The men pulled Juan Pablo out of the mud, weak but alive. Two of the boy's older brothers survived the mudslide that destroyed the family home and much of their village. Like 1,000 other survivors, Juan Pablo and his brothers moved into a tent camp after the disaster. "I lost my whole family and I miss them, my mama and my papa," Juan Pablo told visiting reporters.

This satellite image shows Hurricane Mitch on October 26, 1998, shortly before it hit land.

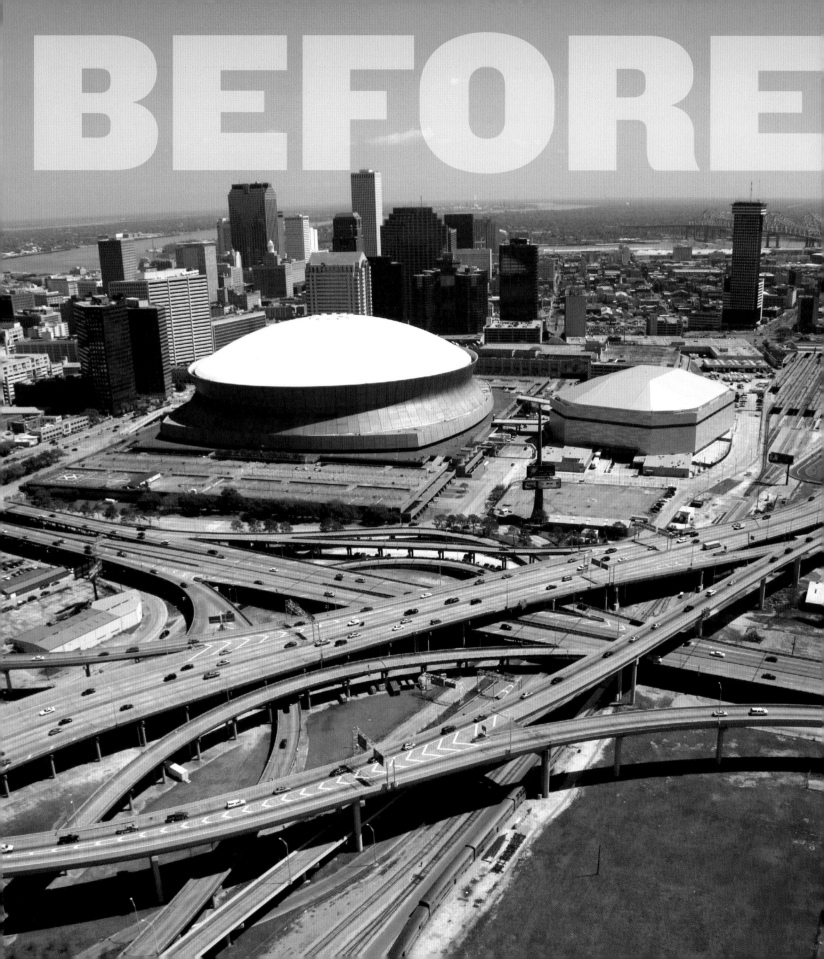

BEFORE

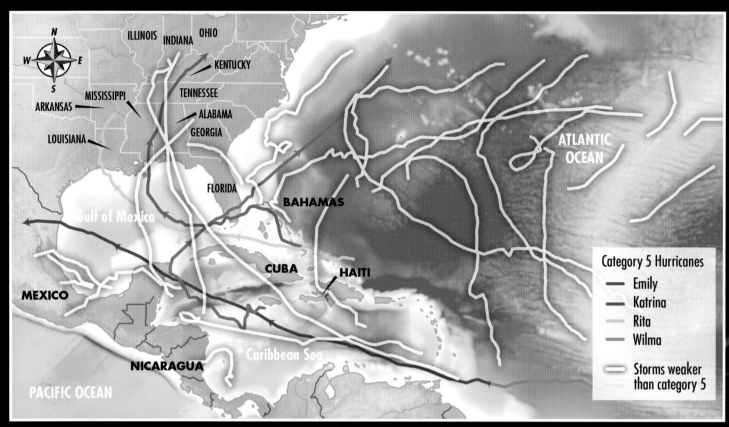

Map labels: ILLINOIS, INDIANA, OHIO, KENTUCKY, TENNESSEE, MISSISSIPPI, ALABAMA, ARKANSAS, GEORGIA, LOUISIANA, FLORIDA, BAHAMAS, Gulf of Mexico, CUBA, HAITI, MEXICO, ATLANTIC OCEAN, Caribbean Sea, NICARAGUA, PACIFIC OCEAN

Category 5 Hurricanes
— Emily
— Katrina
--- Rita
--- Wilma
— Storms weaker than category 5

Katrina alone made the 2005 Atlantic hurricane season a record breaker. But 2005 broke records for breaking records. Here are a few:

- Most named storms in a season: 28
- Most hurricanes in a season: 15
- Most Category 5 hurricanes: 4 (Emily, Katrina, Rita, and Wilma)

- Most major hurricanes (Category 3 and up) to hit the United States: 4 (Dennis, Katrina, Rita, and Wilma)
- Most damage ever recorded in a hurricane season: $150 billion
- Strongest Atlantic hurricane ever: Wilma, 26.05 inHg atmospheric pressure

Costly Katrina

Katrina was the costliest U.S. hurricane ever. With damages totaling at least $85 billion, it is arguably the costliest of any U.S. natural disaster of all time.

Hurricane Katrina

Where: Southeastern Louisiana, southern Mississippi, and southwestern Alabama

When: Gulf Coast landfall on August 29, 2005 • **What:** Category 3 at landfall

How Bad: 1,836 dead; 705 missing

In late August 2005, a growing hurricane named Katrina churned into the Gulf of Mexico. Bahamas-born Katrina had already streaked across the southern tip of Florida, killing seven. By August 28, the warm Gulf water had fueled the storm until it was a Category 5 monster with 175 mph (282km/h) winds. Then, like a predator zeroing in on an easy kill, Katrina turned northwest toward New Orleans, Louisiana.

The half-million residents of New Orleans were in extreme danger. The city sits on land shaped like a bowl. And it's below sea level! New Orleans is also sandwiched between two bodies of water—the Mississippi River to the south and Lake Pontchartrain to the north. The city depends on a complex system of floodwalls, levees, and pumping stations to keep water from filling the bowl.

Early morning on August 29, Katrina slammed into the Gulf Coast as a Category 3 storm. Hurricane conditions reached from southeastern Louisiana through southern Mississippi to southwestern Alabama. Winds gusted up to 125 mph (201km/h), snapping trees, tearing off roofs, and ripping down power lines. Storm surges as high as 34 feet (10m) washed away the seaside sections of Gulf Coast towns, including Mobile, Alabama, and Biloxi, Mississippi.

New Orleans suffered the worst. Katrina's storm surge spilled over and broke through a number of flood barriers. At least 80 percent of "the city in a bowl" flooded. Water filled New Orleans's streets, flooded the entire first floor of homes and buildings, cut off power, and overflowed sewage pipes. Thousands made their way to shelters where too little food and less help fueled chaos and crime. Others waited for days in attics and on rooftops for rescue. People in hospitals and nursing homes had to survive without electricity, safe water, or medicines. As many as 1,500 people died in New Orleans. Television images showed suffering that Americans thought impossible in the United States. Katrina created a catastrophe.

HURRICANE EVACUATION ROUTE

Storm Scientists in Action

Where will the hurricane hit? How strong will it be? These are the two most important questions for a hurricane forecaster. Nothing else matters once a hurricane is on the move. Predicting a hurricane's path—its track—effects where warnings are sent. How strong a storm is—its intensity—decides whether evacuations are necessary. Forecasters save lives by predicting a hurricane's track and intensity. Incorrect forecasts can cost lives.

Tracking the Storm

Figuring out where a hurricane is headed is the easier part. Hurricanes move over the ocean at a sluggish 10–20 mph (16–32km/h). But because they live from three to fourteen days, a hurricane can travel thousands of miles. What steers a hurricane as it cruises over the ocean? The weather around the storm does. Wind patterns and pressure systems can pull a hurricane in one direction—or shove it in another.

Weather-forecasting computers that crunch atmospheric information help calculate a hurricane's track. Meteorologists use the computers' calculations to figure out how surrounding weather will steer a hurricane as it travels. Will westerly winds keep pushing the storm west? Will a high-pressure area move the hurricane north? Good weather-forecasting computers let meteorologists know which is more likely and predict the hurricane's track.

PREDICTING THE PATH

Track error is the distance in miles between a hurricane's real track and its forecasted track. You can see the difference in this track of Hurricane Dennis.

Hurricane Activity
Can I Get a Witness?

Did a hurricane ever roar through your town? Do you know someone who lived through a hurricane? Record the eyewitness account for future generations.

1. **Ask the person to tell his or her story.** You can write it down, record it on a voice recorder, or videotape it.

2. **Ask lots of questions:** How much warning did you have? What were the winds like? When were you most scared? What's the worst thing that happened?

3. **Get some information about the storyteller.** You should include his or her full name, date of birth, place of birth, and the interview date.

4. **Include photocopies or videotape of photographs of the hurricane or its damage, if you can.**

5. **Finished?** Consider donating a copy of your eyewitness account to a local historical society. Future generations will want to know what happened firsthand.

A New Orleans resident stands in his flooded front yard after Hurricane Katrina.

A CATASTROPHIC PATH

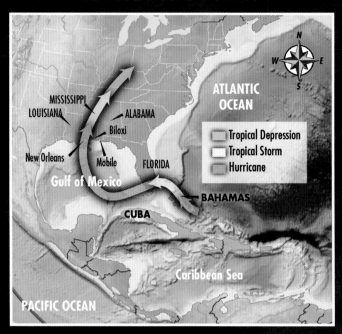

ATLANTIC OCEAN

MISSISSIPPI
LOUISIANA
ALABAMA
Biloxi
New Orleans
Mobile
FLORIDA
Gulf of Mexico
BAHAMAS
CUBA
Caribbean Sea
PACIFIC OCEAN

Tropical Depression
Tropical Storm
Hurricane

Tropical storm Katrina was born in the Caribbean. It became a hurricane as it nicked Florida on its way to the Gulf of Mexico.

Deadly Surge

Katrina had the greatest storm surge from an Atlantic hurricane: 28–30 feet (8.5–9m)

Katrina was the deadliest U.S. hurricane since 1928 and the third deadliest ever.

I WAS THERE!

A Teen Survivor

When Katrina struck New Orleans, water started filling Gerard Broussard's house. The teenager headed to his grandfather's. The older man's home was flooding, too. "I could've left, but I didn't want to leave my grandpa," explained Broussard. "The water at the house started coming up to our thighs, so we went up to the attic and busted a hole in the roof."

The water in the house went down some after the storm passed, so the family decided to try to hold out there. "When we were in my grandpa's house, we had to survive," explained Broussard. "You're a looter when you're taking stuff you don't need. You're a survivor when you're taking stuff you need to survive. I took some sardines and canned goods.... I was trying to find water. Once I got water, we were straight. There was eight of us in the house; we had to live."

After more than a week in the flooded house, Broussard and his family decided to leave. They waded through knee-deep water to the convention center. From there, they were evacuated out of the city.

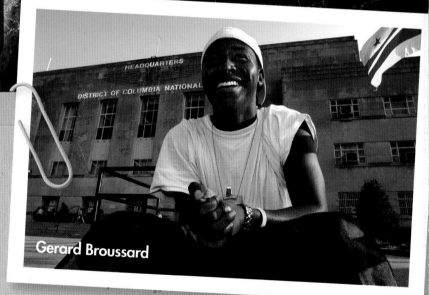

Gerard Broussard

HURRICANE EVACUATION ROUTE

37

Hurricane Hunting

Knowing how strong a hurricane will be at landfall is harder to figure out than its track. Why? Measuring a raging hurricane isn't easy! For meteorologists to predict a storm's strength at landfall, they need to take up-close weather measurements again and again as the hurricane travels. That way, they can tell if it's becoming stronger or weaker.

How do you take the temperature of a gigantic ocean storm? How can you measure its dangerous winds? You climb into an airplane, fasten your seatbelt, and fly right into the swirling storm. It might seem crazy, but that's what meteorologists do. Rugged "Hurricane Hunter" airplanes are packed with weather measuring equipment that meteorologists take right into the storm. While pilots crisscross their planes back and forth across a hurricane, instruments attached to the outside of the planes measure wind speeds, map clouds, and take temperatures.

When Hurricane Hunters reach a hurricane's eye, it's probe-launching time. An onboard meteorologist grabs the special tube-shaped probe, called a dropsonde, and drops it into a chute that opens to the outside. The dropsonde falls through the storm, floating down with the help of its parachute. It measures air pressure, temperature, humidity, wind speed, and wind direction all the way down to the sea. The tough little dropsonde's radio sends all the hurricane weather information back to the meteorologist onboard the bucking airplane.

Hurricane hunting airplanes are tough aircraft packed with special weather-measuring equipment. On the outside of the aircraft are three sets of radar equipment. The radars in the nose, belly, and tail [labeled] give the crew a picture of the weather all around the plane. Four engines [labeled] plow the airplane through the storm. Inside the airplane is high-tech weather-measuring equipment and lots of computers. Dropsondes are released through a chute near the back of the plane.

Hurricane Hunter

Flight crew station

Dropsonde station

Meteorologist stations

Radar

Radar

Radar dish

Engines (2 per wing)

Dropsonde

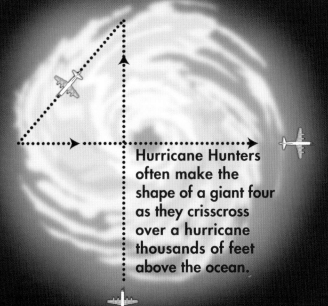

Hurricane Hunters often make the shape of a giant four as they crisscross over a hurricane thousands of feet above the ocean.

Dropsonde

It takes only minutes for a dropsonde to reach the ocean from an airplane flying 10,000 feet (3,048m) high.

Parachute

GPS Antenna

Pressure sensor

Radio transmitter

Humidity and pressure sensors

I WAS THERE!
Trapped in the Eye of Hugo

On September 15, 1989, a crew of National Oceanic and Atmospheric Association (NOAA) Hurricane Hunters flew into Category 3 Hurricane Hugo. Onboard was flight meteorologist Jeff Masters. He'd signed up with the Hurricane Hunters because "I love seeing cool weather phenomena. And the hurricane is the ultimate cool weather phenomena."

Jeff Masters

The crew heading into Hugo wanted to get a close-up first look. So the airplane headed toward Hugo's eye at a low 1,500 feet (457m) above the ocean surface. It's rougher down low, but everyone figured it was safe in a weak Category 3 hurricane.

"About 15 seconds into the eyewall we knew that this was going to be stronger than we expected," said Masters. "It immediately got really dark." Dark clouds dumped drumming rain onto the airplane. Less than a minute later, the airplane was smacked with 155–160 mph (249–257km/h) winds! Hugo was really a monster Category 5 storm. Masters and the crew were smashed down into their seats—and then jerked upward in free fall! A computer, an ice chest, and a 200-pound (91kg) life raft ripped away from their tie-down straps and crashed around the cabin. Screwdrivers, soda cans, silverware, and other debris became flying missiles. "Our number three engine exploded into flames and conked out," said Masters. "The pilots lost control of the aircraft and we went plunging down toward the ocean."

"It's amazing the aircraft survived. Because the wings are supposed to tear off at 6 Gs [gravities of acceleration] and we hit 5½ Gs." Luckily, the airplane coasted forward enough to break through into the calm eye. There the pilots were able to put out the engine fire and take back control of the airplane.

Once in the calm eye, Masters had time to look around. He said it was like being at the bottom of a big spooky stadium looking up. "You're surrounded on all sides by a cylinder of dark clouds," he said. "Everybody was deathly quiet on the airplane," said Masters. Everyone knew the only way out was back through that eyewall again. But the airplane was down to only three engines. Masters figured they had about "a one in three chance" of making it out okay.

The crew knew that if they could get up higher, the eyewall would be less fierce. So the pilot flew the limping airplane in a tight spiral up the eye. That move put them at 6,000 feet (1,829m). From there an Air Force Hurricane Hunter airplane came to their rescue. The Air Force aircraft punched back and forth through the eyewall at different places. Finally, it found a weaker spot that the damaged NOAA craft could use. With their fuel running low, the crew strapped in and popped safely through the eyewall into sunshine. "Hallelujah, the sun is out and we're going home!" remembered Masters.

An Eye for An Eye

What makes a hurricane over the ocean suddenly strengthen—or fade? That's the question ocean-weather expert Shuyi Chen tries to answer. Chen worked on RAINEX—the hurricane Rainband and Intensity Change Experiment of 2005. RAINEX picked a good year for studying hurricanes up close. They studied Hurricanes Katrina, Ophelia, and Rita. Katrina and Rita were both Category 5 storms! "We'd never have imagined we'd have two Category 5 storms," says Chen.

RAINEX scientists outfitted three Hurricane Hunter aircraft with high-definition radar. Then they sent them into hurricanes—all at the same time! The meteorologist team on the ground in Miami, Florida, studied the information coming from the aircraft bouncing through the hurricanes. "The airborne radar data comes into our operations center in real time," explains Chen. By studying the storm in real time, scientists could then send the airplanes exactly where they wanted more measurements. "It's the first time we have ever tried this new way of communicating from the ground to planes flying in a hurricane," says Chen.

RAINEX scientists got to watch Hurricane Rita. The hurricane grew from a Category 1 storm to a Category 5 in less than a day. Why? Rita sucked up moist, warm water fuel from the Gulf of Mexico. Later, Rita's winds dropped from 171 to 112 mph (275 to 180km/h)—the storm had weakened. Why? What happened? A phenomenon called eyewall replacement is what weakened Rita. Rainbands about 12 miles (19km) from the storm's center had formed a solid ring—a new outer eyewall. The wider outer eyewall had the old inner eyewall surrounded. It soon sucked up the fuel from the old eyewall's thunderclouds, causing the inner eyewall to break up. Eyewall replacement like this often temporarily saps a hurricane's strength. Meteorologists knew that—but no one had seen it happening before. "We can see very clearly now what's going on with the hurricane eye," Shuyi Chen says.

RAINEX scientists got to watch Hurricane Rita replace its eyewall in real time! This is what it looked like:

Stage 1

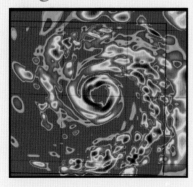

In Stage 1 you can see the hurricane's original inner eyewall and its orange bands of heavy rain and wind.

Stage 2

Stage 2 shows the old eyewall weakening as rainbands begin to form a new thicker, wider, outer eyewall. The new eyewall wraps around the old one and sucks away the old eyewall's energy.

Stage 3

The old inner eyewall is completely gone in Stage 3. The new eyewall begins to tighten as the storm gets ready to strengthen.

Studying Hurricanes from Space

J. Marshall Shepherd has never flown on a Hurricane Hunter mission. "I'm not that crazy," he jokes. The scientist has a different way of "flying into" these huge storms. He stands in front of a computer's satellite picture of a hurricane while putting on 3-D goggles. Then Shepherd touches the satellite picture with an electronic pen. The image zooms in, and reveals an amazing sight. It's not the familiar flat white swirl of clouds, like most satellite pictures. Instead it's three-dimensional and in color. The rainbands look like clusters of tall blue and red towers. The colors of the cloud towers tell their temperature—red is the hottest.

These amazing images come from 250 miles (402km) above Earth. The Tropical Rainfall Measuring Mission (TRMM) is a one-of-a-kind satellite. It not only takes pictures, but also has weather radar onboard. TRMM's radar takes 3-D images of a storm's insides. It reveals a hurricane's towering clouds and their cool blue or hot red temperatures.

"When we see these hot towers, we think that they are giving us a clue that the storm is releasing a lot of energy," explains Shepherd. "And that may be a sign that the storm is about to undergo intensification processes [become stronger]." It's another clue in the mystery of what makes one hurricane strengthen and another weaken. Solving that mystery will help predict how powerful a hurricane will be at landfall—and better prepare those in its path.

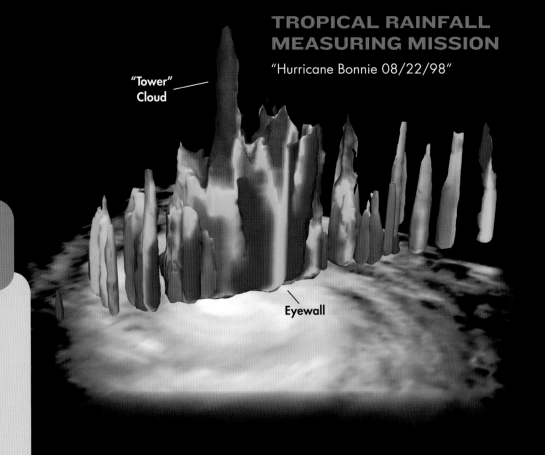

TROPICAL RAINFALL MEASURING MISSION
"Hurricane Bonnie 08/22/98"

"Tower" Cloud

Eyewall

3-D Storm Images from Space

The Tropical Rainfall Measuring Mission (TRMM) satellite is a joint project of the U.S. National Aeronautics and Space Administration (NASA) and the Japanese Space Agency. The rocket carrying TRMM launched from Tanegashima, Japan.

Hurricane Safety

Do you live or visit where hurricanes happen? Being prepared makes all the difference when it comes to storm survival. How can you be ready for the world's biggest storms? Learn what the different weather alerts mean, make a family plan, and put together an emergency kit.

STAY ALERT! BE WARNED!

Weather Alert	What It Means	What to Do
TROPICAL STORM WATCH or **HURRICANE WATCH**	Tropical storm* or hurricane** conditions are possible within 36 hours.	• Pay attention to TV and radio weather reports of the storm's progress. • Stock up on canned food, stored drinking water, extra cash, batteries, first-aid supplies, and plywood for covering windows. • Fill the car's gas tank and charge cell-phone batteries. • Bring in outside stuff that might blow away, such as lawn furniture, garbage cans, etc. • PLAN TO LEAVE if you're in a mobile home or high-rise building, on the coast or an offshore island, or near a river or flood-prone area.
TROPICAL STORM WARNING or **HURRICANE WARNING**	Tropical storm* or hurricane** conditions are expected in 24 hours or less.	• Cover windows and close storm shutters *before* the storm hits. • Listen to TV, radio, or weather radio broadcasts for storm updates and evacuation orders. • LEAVE IMMEDIATELY if in an unsafe building, flood-prone area, or if told to by officials. • During the storm, stay in a room away from windows. • Watch for tornadoes and flooding creeks and rivers—steer clear of both. Wind and waves aren't the only hazards of hurricanes.

* Tropical storm conditions include 39–73 mph (63–117km/h) winds, high waves, and flooding.

**Hurricane conditions include 74 mph (119km/h) and higher winds, dangerously high water, or high waves.

>> **Don't** stay in a mobile home during a hurricane.

>> **Do** plan for your pets. Know where they are and have pet carriers on hand. Know which shelters or motels allow pets.

>> **Don't** be fooled! Often winds suddenly die down as the eye passes over, but they'll soon pick up again.

>> **Do** let relatives and neighbors know if you're evacuating.

BEFORE

AFTER

The front stairs of the Dome of a Home are meant to break away during a storm. This lets water flow under the house, instead of pushing it over.

I WAS THERE!
Ivan vs. Home Sweet Dome

Hurricane Ivan killed fifty Americans, cut off electricity in fourteen states, and caused flooding as far north as Ohio. But Pensacola, Florida, took the biggest hit when the Category 3 storm made landfall near the Alabama-Florida border. The storm's 130 mph (209km/h) winds, heavy rain, and giant storm surge flooded the entire downtown. The 2004 hurricane also collapsed a highway bridge.

Mark Sigler watched the hurricane come ashore from his beach house. "Those were the biggest waves I'd ever seen," said Sigler. "I couldn't believe what I was seeing." But Sigler didn't run away. He stayed in his home all night as the winds and storm surge ripped up and washed away his neighbors' houses. Sigler even heard "huge chunks of other houses bouncing off of" his house during the storm.

Why did Sigler's home survive? His so-called Dome of a Home was designed to survive hurricanes. Its dome-shape has no edges for the wind to catch. The windows are made of super-strong glass. The home also sits on top of strong poles sunk deep into the ground. So storm surge water flows under the house, instead of plowing it over.

The morning after Ivan, Sigler came out of his dome to a wrecked world. About 80 percent of the homes on Pensacola Beach were destroyed. "It was overwhelming," said Sigler about the destruction. But the Dome of a Home was fine. Sigler thinks buildings built in hurricane areas need to be stronger. He built his dome to show that homes can be hurricane proof. Hurricane Ivan helped him prove his point.

BIBLIOGRAPHY

Carson, Mary Kay. *Weather Projects for Young Scientists*. Chicago: Chicago Review Press, 2007.

Fitzpatrick, Patrick J. *Natural Disasters: Hurricanes*. Santa Barbara: ABC-CLIOs, 1999.

Graham, Steve and Holli Riebeek. "Hurricanes: The Greatest Storms on Earth." *Earth Observatory,* November 1, 2006. http://earthobservatory.nasa.gov/Features/Hurricanes/.

"Hurricane Preparedness Week." National Hurricane Center Web Site. http://www.nhc.noaa.gov/HAW2/english/intro.shtml.

"Hurricanes: Unleashing Nature's Fury." A Preparedness Guide from U.S. Department of Commerce, National Oceanic and Atmospheric Association, and National Weather Service. http://www.nws.noaa.gov/om/hurricane/pdfs/HurricanesUNF07.pdf.

Norcross, Bryan. *Hurricane Almanac: The Essential Guide to Storms Past, Present, and Future*. New York: St. Martin's Griffin, 2007.

"Online Meteorology Guide: Hurricanes." WW2010: University of Illinois Web Site. http://ww2010.atmos.uiuc.edu/%28Gh%29/guides/mtr/hurr/home.rxml.

Williams, Jack. *The Weather Book: An Easy-to-Understand Guide to the USA's Weather*. New York: Vintage, 1997.

SOURCE NOTES

PAGE 18: "If there is . . . in hurricane activity,": Michael Cabbage, "Warming heats up hurricane debate: Are rising temperatures creating more-intense Atlantic storm seasons?" *Knight Ridder/Tribune Business News* (Washington, February 14, 2007), 1.

PAGE 18: "If global warming . . . the overall system.": Juliet Eilperin, "Hurricane Scientist Leaves U.N. Team: U.S. Expert Cites Politics in a Letter," *Washington Post* (January 23, 2005), A13.

PAGE 18: "Sea-surface temperatures . . . of global warming,": Michael Cabbage, "Warming heats up hurricane debate: Are rising temperatures creating more-intense Atlantic storm seasons?" *Knight Ridder/Tribune Business News* (Washington: February 14, 2007), 1.

PAGE 18: "When it rains . . . few years ago,": "Hurricane Predictors Expect a Busy Storm Season," *All Things Considered* (Washington, D.C.: May 22, 2007), 1.

PAGE 28: "We heard the . . . stereos and couches.": Rachel Catz, "105 minutes of hurricane terror series," X-PRESSIONS, *St. Petersburg Times* (Florida: August 12, 1996), 4.D.

PAGE 28: "I couldn't believe . . . for two days.": Rachel Catz, "105 minutes of hurricane terror series," X-PRESSIONS, *St. Petersburg Times* (Florida: August 12, 1996), 4.D.

PAGE 29: "The roofs . . . flying timbers.": Isaac M. Cline, "Special Report On The Galveston Hurricane Of September 8, 1900," http://www.history.noaa.gov/stories_tales/cline2.html.

PAGE 29: "My residence . . . drifting to sea.": Isaac M. Cline, "Special Report On The Galveston Hurricane Of September 8, 1900," http://www.history.noaa.gov/stories_tales/cline2.html.

PAGE 31: "I lost my . . . and my papa,": "Clinton Meets with Survivors of Hurricane Mitch," [FIRST Edition] *Seattle Times* (Washington: March 9, 1999), A.7.

PAGE 37: "I could've left . . . in the roof.": "Teen Survivors of Hurricane Katrina Share Their Stories," (September 12, 2005), http://www.pbs.org/newshour/extra/features/july-dec05/survivors_9-12.html.

PAGE 37: "When we were . . . had to live.": "Teen Survivors of Hurricane Katrina Share Their Stories," (September 12, 2005), http://www.pbs.org/newshour/extra/features/july-dec05/survivors_9-12.html.

PAGE 40: "I love seeing . . . cool weather phenomena." "Hurricane Hunters: Interview with Jeff Masters," *The Story* (American Public Media: June, 1, 2007), http://thestory.org/archive/.

PAGE 40: "About 15 seconds . . . toward the ocean.": "Hurricane Hunters: Interview with Jeff Masters," *The Story* (American Public Media: June, 1, 2007), http://thestory.org/archive/.

PAGE 40: "It's amazing . . . hit 5½ Gs.": "Hurricane Hunters: Interview with Jeff Masters." *The Story* (American Public Media: June, 1, 2007), http://thestory.org/archive/.

PAGE 40: "You're surrounded . . . on the airplane.": "Hurricane Hunters: Interview with Jeff Masters," *The Story* (American Public Media: June, 1, 2007), http://thestory.org/archive/.

PAGE 40: "Hallelujah, the sun . . . we're going home!": "Hurricane Hunters: Interview with Jeff Masters," *The Story* (American Public Media: June, 1, 2007), http://thestory.org/archive/.

PAGE 41: "We'd never have . . . Category 5 storms,": Theresa Bradley, "Researchers Unravel Storm," *Miami Herald* (Florida, September 27, 2009), 3B.

PAGE 41: "The airborne radar . . . in a hurricane,": "Imaging Helps Hurricane Endeavors," (October 20, 2005), http://www.advancedimagingpro.com/print/Advanced-Imaging-Magazine/Imaging-Helps-Hurricane-Endeavors/1$1924.

PAGE 41: "We can see . . . the hurricane eye,": "Science Notes," *Buffalo News* (Buffalo, New York: March 11, 2007), I6.

PAGE 42: "I'm not that crazy,": "Science Now. Ask the Expert: Marshall Shepherd," (October 20, 2005), http://www.pbs.org/wgbh/nova/sciencenow/3214/06-ask.html.

PAGE 42: "When we see . . . undergo intensification processes.": "Hurricanes," *NOVA scienceNOW* Transcript (January 25, 2005), http://www.pbs.org/wgbh/nova/transcripts/3204_sciencen.html#h02.

PAGE 44: "Those were the . . . bouncing off of": "Hurricane Summer," *National Geographic Presents*, October 2004.

PAGE 44: "It was overwhelming,": "Hurricane Summer," *National Geographic Presents,* October 2004.

Find Out More

WEB SITES TO VISIT

National Hurricane Center
www.nhc.noaa.gov
Besides the most up-to-date information on current storms, this site has tracking charts you can download, print out, and use to plot where a storm is by noting the longitude and latitude positions regularly posted on the Web site. Connect the dots and track the storm yourself.

FEMA for Kids
www.fema.gov/kids/hurr.htm
The Federal Emergency Management Agency's site for kids about preparing for a hurricane. Get in the know and get ready!

Hurricane Hunters
www.hurricanehunters.com
Learn more about the bravest meteorologists of all.

Hurricane Storm Science
www.miamisci.org/hurricane/
Miami Museum of Science brings you a site full of hurricane facts.

Climate Change Kids Site
www.epa.gov/climatechange/kids/
Find out more about climate change—and what to do about it—at this Environmental Protection Agency Web site.

DVDS TO WATCH

How to Stop a Hurricane. Dir. Robin Benger. (Tremendous Media, 2009).

Savage Planet: Storms of the Century. Dir. Emma Hawley, Kate Coombs. (Orland Park, IL: MPI Home Video, 2007).

Hurricane!: Katrina, Gilbert and Camille. NOVA. (South Burlington, MA: WGBH Boston

HURRICANE TRACKER WORDS TO KNOW

ATMOSPHERIC PRESSURE also called air pressure; the weight of the air from the ground (or water's surface) to the top of the atmosphere

BAROMETER an instrument that measures atmospheric pressure, often given in inches of mercury (inHg)

CYCLONE a tropical cyclone in the Indian Ocean with winds of at least 74 mph (119 km/h)

EYE the calm and rain-free center of a hurricane

EYEWALL the ring of tall thunderstorm clouds surrounding the eye, also called a wall cloud

HURRICANES tropical cyclones on either side of the Americas with winds of at least 74 mph (119km/h)

RADAR short for **ra**dio **d**etecting and **r**anging; it's a technology for detecting distant objects, including rain, clouds, and storms

RAINBAND bands of packed thunderstorm clouds in a tropical cyclone

STORM SURGE a rise in sea level underneath a hurricane from winds and low pressure

STORM TIDE storm surge height with normal tide added

TROPICAL CYCLONE powerful, rotating ocean storm with high winds

TROPICAL DEPRESSION a tropical cyclone with winds of 38 mph (61km/h) or less

TROPICAL DISTURBANCE a moving weather system over a tropical ocean that lasts for more than 24 hours, isn't moving due to two different air masses colliding (a front), and may develop into a tropical depression

TROPICAL STORMS tropical cyclones with winds of 39–73 mph (63–117km/h)

TYPHOON a tropical cyclone in the northern Pacific Ocean with winds of at least 74 mph (119km/h)

WIND SHEAR the difference in wind speed and/or direction between two short distances

INDEX

2005 Hurricane records, 25, 33
Activities
  building barometer, 20
  preparing for hurricane, 47
  recording eyewitness account, 36
Andrew, Hurricane, 27–28
Atmospheric (air) pressure
  for Category 1 to 5 hurricanes, 23–24
  changes explained, 20
  defined, 20, 45
  low, inside hurricane, 20, 21
  measuring, making barometer for, 20
  storm surges and, 17
Barometers, 20, 45
Bhola, Cyclone, 17
Broussard Gerard, 37
Catarina, Hurricane, 8
Category 1 to 5 defined, 22–24
Catz, Rachel, 28
Chen, Shuyi, 41
Climate change, 18
Cline, Isaac, 29
Coriolis effect, 13
Costly hurricanes, 26, 28, 33
Cyclones, defined, 5, 45. See also Tropical cyclones
Damage. See also Katrina, Hurricane
  by category (1 to 5) of hurricane, 23–24
  dome-shaped house to avoid, 44
  Galveston Hurricane, 26, 29
  Hurricane Andrew, 27–28
  Hurricane Mitch, 30–31
  photographs of, 19, 23–24, 26, 28, 30–31, 35, 36
  safety precautions to avoid, 43, 47
Deadliest hurricanes, 29, 30
Development of hurricanes
  heat, wind, water and, 11
  hurricane declared, 15
  looking inside, 16–17
  mechanics of, 11–16, 21
  reason for rotation, 13

tropical depression stage, 7, 13, 17, 45
tropical disturbance stage, 11, 12, 45
tropical storm stage, 7, 14, 17, 22, 43, 45
Direction of hurricane/wind, 13, 16, 17
Dome of a Home, 44
Dropsondes, 39
Energy of hurricanes, 9, 10
Eye, 15, 16, 17, 20, 39, 40, 41, 45
Eyewall, 16, 40, 41, 42, 45
Forecasting hurricanes. See also Tracking hurricanes
  computers for, 38
  deadly error in Galveston, 29
Galveston Hurricane, 26, 29
Geography of hurricanes, 6–7
Global warming, 18
Heat
  of air and water mixing, 11, 16–17
  climate change and, 18
  creating hurricanes, 11–16, 21
  of seawater fueling hurricanes, 5, 8, 10
House, to survive hurricanes, 44
Hugo, Hurricane, 40
Hurricane Hunter airplanes, 39–41
Hurricanes
  about: overview of, 4
  defined, 45
  parameters defining, 15
  scientific name. See Tropical cyclones
  word origin, 5
Hurricane watch and warning, 43
Ingredients of hurricanes, 11
Ivan, Hurricane, 44
Katrina, Hurricane, 32–37
  before and after photos, 34–35
  cost of, 28, 33
  description and statistics, 32, 33, 37
  path of, 37
  photographs of damage, 19, 35, 36
  storm surge of, 19, 32, 37

teen survivor's account, 37
temperature of seawater fueling, 10
2005 hurricane records and, 25, 33
Lifespan of hurricanes, 38
Locations of hurricanes, 6–7
Mitch, Hurricane, 30–31
Naming/names of hurricanes, 25. See also specific names
Nargis, Cyclone, 5
Narvaez, Juan Pablo Montoya, 31
Preparing for hurricane, 47. See also Safety guidelines
Pressure. See Atmospheric (air) pressure
Radar, 39, 41, 42, 45
Rain
  amount generated, 10
  from Hurricane Mitch, 30–31
  Tropical Rainfall Measuring Mission (TRMM), 42
Rainbands, 16, 17, 41, 42, 45
RAINEX project, 41
Rating hurricanes. See Strength of hurricanes
Recording eyewitness account, 36
Resources, 45–46
Retired names of hurricanes, 25
Rita, Hurricane, 41
Rotation, reason for, 13
Safety guidelines, 43, 47
Saffir, Herbert, 22
Saffir-Simpson Scale, 22–24
Season for hurricanes, 8
Seawater
  climate change and, 18
  storm surges, 17
  temperature of, 5, 8, 10
Sigler, Mark, 44
Simpson, Bob, 22
Space, tracking hurricanes from, 42
Storm surges, 17, 19, 23–24, 26, 32, 33, 44, 45
Storm tide, 17, 26, 45
Strength of hurricanes
  Category 1 to 5 defined, 22–24
  measuring in airplane, 39–41

tropical cyclone paths illustrated, 7–8
wind speed and, 15, 22
Temperature
  climate change and, 18
  of seawater fueling hurricanes, 5, 8, 10
3-D Storm images, 42
Thunderstorms, 15
Tower clouds, 42
Track error, 38
Tracking hurricanes, 38–42
  about: overview of, 38
  dropsondes and, 39
  Hurricane Hunter airplanes for, 39–41
  RAINEX project, 41
  from space, 42
  trapped in eye of Hugo, 40
Trenberth, Kevin, 18
Tropical cyclones
  map showing paths of all, 7–8
  other names for, 6
  as scientific name for hurricanes, 5
Tropical depressions, 7, 13, 17, 45
Tropical disturbances, 11, 12, 45
Tropical Rainfall Measuring Mission (TRMM), 42
Tropical storms, 7, 14, 17, 22, 43, 45
Tropical storm watch and warning, 43
Typhoons, 6, 7, 8, 10, 25, 45
Watches and warnings, safety guidelines, 43
Winds
  for Category 1 to 5 hurricanes, 23–24
  converging, 11
  creating hurricanes, 11–16, 21
  directions of, 13, 16, 17
  dome-shaped house and, 44
  speed of hurricanes, 15, 22, 23–24
  speed of tropical depressions, 13
  speed of tropical storms, 14
Wind shear, 11, 18, 28, 45

Hurricane Activity
Get It Together

The best time to figure out what to do during a hurricane is before the storm starts. Here's how to get ready:

1. **Put together a hurricane kit:** bottled water, food that doesn't need to be refrigerated (cans, etc.), first-aid supplies, flashlight, battery or crank-powered radio or weather radio, rain ponchos, and sleeping bags or blankets.

2. **Make a family plan—and practice it.**
   - **Know where to go.** Map out a safe evacuation route that avoids flood-prone roads. (Roads in many coastal towns are marked with hurricane-evacuation route signs.) Find out where the nearest public hurricane shelter is.
   - **Hurricane Watch List.** Make a check list of what to get together during a hurricane watch, in case it becomes a warning. Make sure your hurricane kit is complete.
   - **Hurricane Drill.** Practice your evacuation route as well as the way to the nearest shelter.

3. **Post your Hurricane Watch List somewhere easy to see.**

AWE-Inspiring Storms

Hurricanes are a force of nature, forged by an ocean-covered planet and fueled by sun-warmed seawater. Scientists are learning more and more about what drives, strengthens, and steers these worldwide weather events. As meteorologists uncover more hurricane secrets, predictions of storm paths and intensity will improve. This will give coastal communities more time to prepare, saving lives. Want to keep learning about hurricanes? Flip up this page to Find Out More!

HURRICANE
EVACUATION
ROUTE